REALLY ROTTEN JOKES

THE BEANObooks

geddes & grosset

What has two humps and is found at the North Pole?

A lost camel!

Which word is always spelled wrongly?

Wrongly!

2

3

Why does a glow worm glow?

It only eats light meals.

WAITER! This pancake tastes awful!

That's because you've just eaten the paper plate, sir!

Why is a fishmonger never generous! *Because his business makes him sell fish.*

What do sad fir trees do?
They *pine a lot!*

What two words have
the most letters?
Post Office.

Why is an author the
queerest animal in the
world?
*Because his tale comes
out of his head!*

What is the difference between an oak tree and a tight boot?

One makes acorns, the other makes corns ache.

What is bought by the metre and worn by the foot?

A carpet.

What can you keep after giving it to someone else?

Your word.

My grandfather is over eighty and he hasn't a grey hair in his head. Incredible!

No, he's bald!

14

Which bird never runs but is always out of breath?
A puffin!

WISH I WAS OLD ENOUGH TO WASH MY OWN FACE!

WHY'S 'AT?

'COS THEN I WOULDN'T BOTHER!

15

What lies on the ground, a hundred feet up in the air?
A centipede on its back.

19

21

Did you hear about the teacher who was cross-eyed?
He couldn't control his pupils.

Why is a giraffe a big eater?
Because he makes a little go a long way.

When is a clock on the stairs really dangerous?

When it runs down and strikes one.

What is yellow and goes clicketty-click?

A ball-point banana.

What do liars do when they die?

They lie still.

Why does Fido turn round so often before sitting down? *He's a watch dog. He's winding himself up.*

Why doesn't Sweden send her cattle abroad? *Because she keeps her STOCK-holm.*

What makes more noise than a cat stuck up a tree?
Two cats stuck up a tree.

Why are church bells like naughty children?

Because they are never silent when they are tolled.

What is a bad-tempered custard?

One that is upset over trifles.

Can you name a word with five
letters which, if you take two letters
away, leaves one?
ST-ONE.

What pets are made of wood?
PUP-pets.

Why does a school playground get bigger when school starts?

It has more feet in it!

What is white when it's dirty and black when it's clean?

A blackboard!

40

44

Doctor! Doctor! I feel like a pair of scissors.
Well, you can cut that out right now.

49

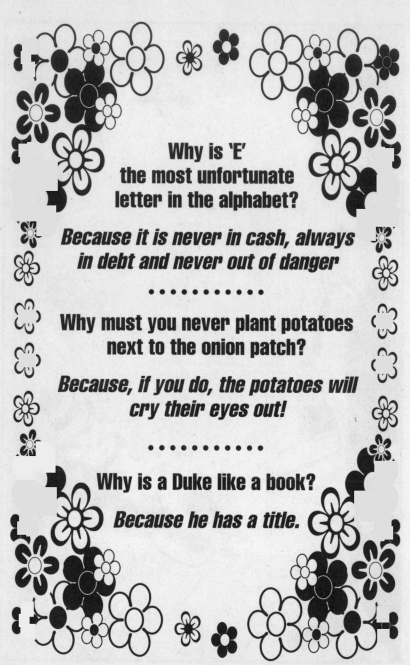

**Why is 'E'
the most unfortunate
letter in the alphabet?**

*Because it is never in cash, always
in debt and never out of danger*

. . . .

**Why must you never plant potatoes
next to the onion patch?**

*Because, if you do, the potatoes will
cry their eyes out!*

. . . .

Why is a Duke like a book?

Because he has a title.

What makes the tower of Pisa lean?

It never eats!

Where do you take a sick horse?

To a HORSEpital!

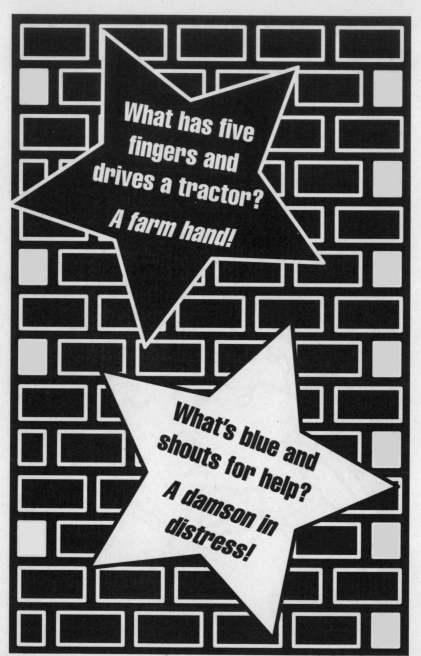

What should you eat before a race?
Runner beans.

. . . .

Why is a farmer clever?
Because he can turn a cow into a field.

1st Cannibal — Am I late for supper?
2nd Cannibal — Yes, everyone's eaten.

Why is a sum like a waxworks show? Because they are both full of figures.

What do you get when you pour boiling water down a rabbit hole?
Hot cross bunnies!

"Where is the English Channel?"
"I don't know. We can't get it on our television."

If a butcher weighs 12 stones when his shop is shut, what does he weigh when it's open? *Meat.*

What do you get if you cross a sheep, a cow and a baby goat? *The Milky Baa Kid.*

What do aliens use to cook their dinner? *Frying saucers!*

Why did the cow jump over the moon? *Because the milkmaid had cold hands.*

What's French, very tall and wobbles!
The Trifle Tower!

Who sings at big hotels?
Hilton John!

How should you dress on a cold day?
As quickly as possible.

A man went to town on Tuesday, stayed overnight and came back in the morning on Tuesday. How come?
He had a horse called Tuesday.

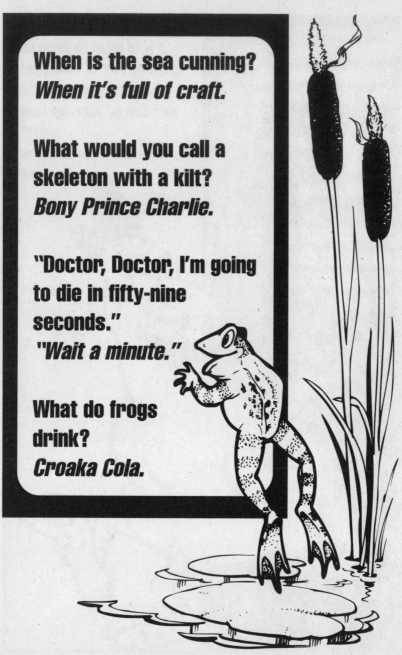

When is the sea cunning?
When it's full of craft.

What would you call a
skeleton with a kilt?
Bony Prince Charlie.

"Doctor, Doctor, I'm going
to die in fifty-nine
seconds."
"Wait a minute."

What do frogs
drink?
Croaka Cola.

64

What are you if your mum's from Iceland and your dad's from Cuba?
An ice-cube!

What does a pilot have to do before he is considered professional?
Qualifly!

Did you hear about the deaf fish . . . ?
. . . He wore a herring aid!

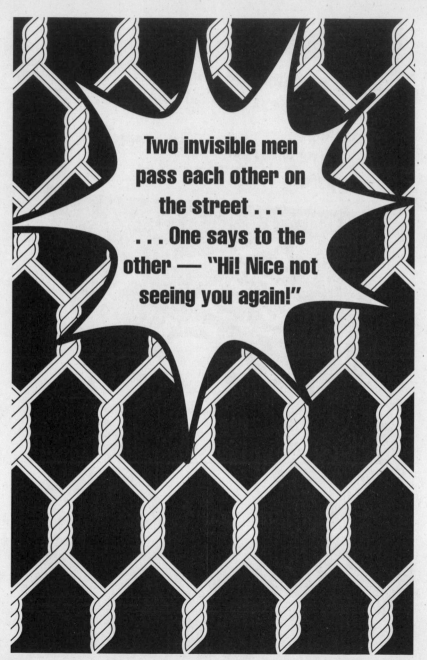

How do you get sick pigs to hospital?
Easy — in a HAMbulance.

....

What do vampires eat at the interval?
ReFLESHments!

"Doctor, Doctor, I'm so fed up."
"Well, don't eat so much."
. . . .
Did you hear about the man who had to go to hospital after eating daffodil bulbs?
He'll be out next spring!

"Waiter! This fish isn't as good as the one I had last week."

"That's odd! It's the same fish."

What's the difference between a well-dressed man and a tired dog? *One wears a suit, the other just pants!*

Why are elephants grey and wrinkled? *Cos they're difficult to wash and iron!*

Smiffy keeps an empty milk bottle in the fridge
. . . in case anyone wants black coffee.

. . . .

What do you call a camel with three humps?
Humphthree!

What kind of clapping do you hear at Christmas time?
Santapplause!

What games do horses play best?
Stable-tennis!

What do you get if you cross a pig with a flea?
Pork scratchings!

What do you get if you cross a hedgehog with a giraffe?
An eight foot toothbrush!

How does an Eskimo
make his house?
Igloos it together!

What do you give a
constipated budgie?
Chirrup of figs!

What do you get if
you cross Dumbo
with a ghost?
An Elephantom!

How do you score
500 at darts?
Throw a hedgehog!

What did the fleas do when they won the lottery?
Bought a dog in Spain!

My baby brother does bird impressions . . .
he eats worms!

How do you stop a cold going to your chest?
Tie a knot in your neck!

What's yellow and comes from Scotland?
The Loch Ness banana!

What's a sick reptile?
An illigator!

If I have £20 in one pocket and £30 in another, what do I have?
Dad's trousers on.

What do you call a donkey with three legs?
A wonkey!

What do you call a lazy cockerel?
A cock-a-doodle don't!

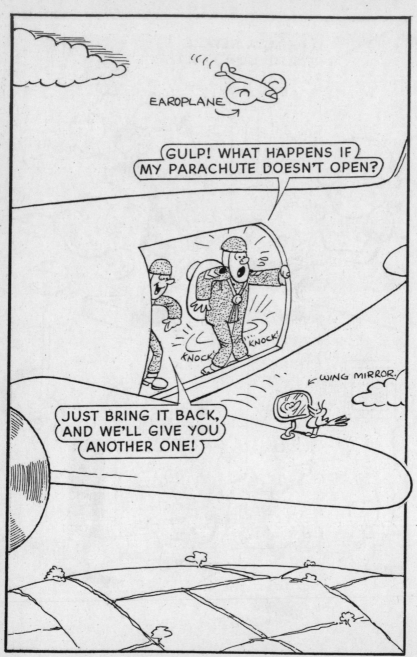